I0423811

Evaluation Report

Report Number: OIG-SBLF-11-002

STATE SMALL BUSINESS CREDIT INITIATIVE: Treasury Needs To Strengthen State Accountability for Use of Funds

Report Date: August 5, 2011

Office of
Inspector General

DEPARTMENT OF THE TREASURY

Contents

Evaluation Report

Appendices

Abbreviations

OIG   Office of Inspector General
OMB   Office of Management and Budget
SSBCI   State Small Business Credit Initiative

OIG

Evaluation

Report

The Department of the Treasury
Office of Inspector General

August 5, 2011

Don Graves, Jr.
Deputy Assistant Secretary for Small Business, Housing, and
Community Development

Since the State Small Business Credit Initiative (SSBCI) was launched
in December 2010, my office has reviewed policy guidance and other
key program documents at your request in advance of their release to
assist you in establishing a strong oversight structure for the SSBCI
program. We believe that seeking our assistance during the
developmental stage of the program illustrates the Department's
commitment to establishing proper controls for monitoring participants
and the expenditure of funds. In general, your office has been
responsive to our suggestions, including modifying the program
application to request data needed to evaluate each applicant's ability
to oversee compliance activities and to safeguard against the misuse
of funds. These and other steps your office has taken should help to
ensure proper accountability over the allocated funds.

This report summarizes our evaluation of the Allocation Agreement
between the Treasury Department and participating States and the
Department's *Guidelines for the State Small Business Credit Initiative*
(policy guidelines). We reviewed the documents[1] to determine whether
Treasury had adequately defined the compliance and oversight
obligations of participating States to establish proper accountability for
oversight of allocated funds.

---

[1] We also reviewed all annexes to the Allocation Agreement, the Frequently Asked
Questions, and the Allocation notice letter.

Before Treasury can disburse funds, it must execute an Allocation Agreement with every participating State that sets forth internal control, compliance and reporting requirements. Among other things, the Allocation Agreement provides that the participating States will comply with Title III of the Small Business Jobs Act (the Act), Treasury regulations and other requirements prescribed pursuant to the Act (including the policy guidelines), applicable provisions of the Grants Management Common Rule, and all applicable Federal, State, and local laws, regulations, ordinances and Office of Management and Budget (OMB) circulars. Therefore, the agreement is the main document for holding program participants accountable for oversight of the use of allocated funds.

Our review identified several areas where SSBCI's compliance and oversight framework could be improved. First, the Allocation Agreement should clearly define the oversight obligations of participating States and specify minimum standards for determining whether participating States have fulfilled their oversight responsibilities. Further, the language in the Allocation Agreement and policy guidelines should require that participating States collect and review compliance assurances made by lenders and borrowers and that all recipients provide compliance assurances. Finally, Treasury should define what constitutes a "material adverse change" in a participating States' condition, financial or otherwise, or operations, which would reduce uncertainty about when a State must notify Treasury. As a result, participating States may not exercise sufficient oversight of funds allocated under the SSBCI program, and Treasury and the Office of Inspector General (OIG) may have difficulty establishing whether participating States are in default of program requirements or have misused funds.

To its credit, Treasury has taken immediate action to address the issues raised in this report. Because only 17 participating States have received funding at this point in the program, the changes Treasury has made and plans to make will strengthen the SSBCI compliance framework in advance of the majority of participating States' receipt of allocated funds.

Background

SSBCI is a $1.5 billion Treasury program created by the Act aimed at increasing access to credit for small businesses. The program gives States, territories and eligible municipalities (referred to by Treasury as participating States) the opportunity to fund Capital Access Programs and Other Credit Support Programs. Capital Access Programs provide portfolio insurance for business loans based on a separate loan loss reserve fund for each participating financial institution. Other Credit Support Programs include collateral support, loan participation, loan guarantee, and venture capital programs. Each participating State is required to designate specific departments, agencies, or political subdivisions to implement the programs approved for funding. The designated State entity distributes the SSBCI funds to various public and private institutions, which may include a subdivision of another State, a for-profit entity supervised by the State, a non-profit entity supervised by the State, or a financial institution. These entities use the funds to make loans or provide credit access to small businesses.

If SSBCI funds are provided to a financial institution in connection with a Capital Access Program, the Act requires the financial institution lender to secure assurances from borrowers that loans made with the funds will not be used for an impermissible purpose or provided to ineligible parties. The SSBCI policy guidelines also extend these requirements to financial institution recipients participating in Other Credit Support Programs. Additionally, each participating State must certify quarterly that it is implementing its programs in accordance with SSBCI program requirements. The Act also requires each financial institution to certify its compliance with SSBCI requirements, and provide assurances that it has verified the identity of borrowers and determined that they have not been convicted of a sex offense against a minor.

Primary oversight of the use of SSBCI funds is the responsibility of each participating State. To ensure that funds are properly controlled and expended, the Act requires that Treasury execute an Allocation Agreement with participants setting forth internal control, compliance and reporting requirements before allocating SSBCI funds. In January 2011, Treasury issued its Allocation Agreement for the SSBCI program. The Allocation Agreement was revised on April 29, 2011, to incorporate policy changes. By signing the agreement, participants agree to comply with policy guidelines governing the use of SSBCI funds, program income, and allowable costs; national standards for internal controls and financial management systems; and other Government requirements. Participating States must also make representations about their legal ability to comply with all applicable agreements and conditions in the Allocation Agreement. Additionally, to receive disbursements of SSBCI funds beyond its initial allocation, participating States are required to certify that they are implementing their approved State programs in accordance with the Act and guidance issued by Treasury; and that the representations and warranties in the Allocation Agreement are true and correct in all material respects.

Expectations for State Oversight of SSBCI Funds Need to Be More Clearly Defined

Treasury guidance requires that participating States supervise contractors and oversee State program(s). Specifically, the policy guidelines require that financial institution lenders of SSBCI funds be accountable to the participating State. However, the guidelines do not define "oversight," "supervision," and "accountability" or specify minimum standards for what the participating States need to do to demonstrate that they have fulfilled their responsibilities in these areas. Because Treasury has not defined these terms, their meaning and significance for the Allocation Agreement and the SSBCI Program are uncertain. This is particularly important because the Act imposes specific requirements and restrictions on the use of SSBCI funds that will require a level of monitoring beyond what the participating States are currently obligated to provide for their Capital Access Programs and Other Credit Support Programs. As a result, the degree to which participating States will monitor compliance with these requirements and restrictions is unclear.

It is also unclear whether oversight by participating States will extend to institution lenders and other participants in the approved State programs. The Act and policy guidelines require lender certifications and borrower assurances that are unique to SSBCI. For example, the Act imposes particular requirements and prohibitions on loans provided under State Capital Access Programs and Other Credit Support Programs, such as prohibiting the use of SSBCI funds to refinance loans previously made to borrowers. However, the Allocation Agreement and policy guidelines do not clearly discuss how the participating States are required to oversee compliance with loan requirements and restrictions. As a result, Treasury appears to be relying solely on lender certifications and borrower assurances to determine compliance with these provisions of the Act.

Additionally, at the time of our review, neither the Allocation Agreement nor the guidelines specified how the designated agencies of the participating States are to ensure that their contractor(s) comply with program requirements, especially when the contractor is a political subdivision of another State over which it may have limited or no oversight authority. According to Treasury officials, if the contractor is not clearly an agency answerable to the designated State agency, it will require the participating State to sign a "waterfall" agreement with the contractor. The waterfall agreement requires the contractor to abide by all covenants, agreements and events of default in the Allocation Agreement. As we were drafting our report, Treasury finalized the waterfall agreement provisions and incorporated them into Annex 1 of the Allocation Agreement. The first waterfall agreement was used on June 28, 2011. While the agreement creates clearer downstream obligations for those parties who are not clearly answerable to State agencies (e.g., non-profits established by a banking consortium in the State), it does not specify what "answerable to" means for purposes of the SSBCI program.

Without clear definitions and expectations for oversight, supervision, and accountability, it is uncertain how Treasury and the OIG will be able to determine that a participating State has failed to exercise oversight authority for purposes of finding the State to be in default of program requirements or that it intentionally or recklessly misused funds. For example, as set forth in the Allocation Agreement, States are required to comply with SSBCI requirements. Treasury may consider a participating State to be in general default if it fails to materially observe, comply with, or meet or perform any term, covenant, agreement or other provision in the Allocation Agreement. Without minimum compliance standards, however, it is unclear whether Treasury would be able to hold a participating State liable for a recipient's actions under the Allocation Agreement, or to determine that the certifications were materially false.

In addition to the general event of default described above, the Allocation Agreement contains a specific event of default, triggered when the OIG finds that a participating State intentionally or recklessly misused allocated funds. Under those circumstances, Treasury would recoup the funds. However, Treasury has not defined "intentional or reckless misuse of allocated funds." Because SSBCI funds pass through the State to recipients of the State programs, misuse of funds would primarily occur at the recipient level. Therefore, to find that a participating State intentionally and recklessly misused SSBCI funds, Treasury would need to provide a clear definition of "intentional or reckless misuse of allocated funds." Without a clear definition, it is unclear how Treasury could recoup the funds from a participating State.

We believe that if the participating State were obligated to adhere to certain standards for oversight of recipients, such as financial institution lenders, the participating State would have the necessary involvement in and awareness of their activities, making it easier to support a finding of "intentional or reckless misuse." However, without setting forth minimum standards, it will be difficult to determine that a participating State intentionally misused funds and had committed a specific event of default. Therefore, at a minimum, Treasury should modify the Allocation Agreement or amend the policy guidelines to require participating States to make a representation that it is aware of, and is monitoring and enforcing compliance with the policy guidelines and other restrictions applicable to program recipients; and define "intentional or reckless misuse of allocated funds."

Participating States Are Not Required to Collect or Review Recipient Assurances of Program Compliance

The language in the Allocation Agreement and policy guidelines are insufficient to hold participating States accountable for ensuring that recipients of SSBCI funds have complied with program requirements. Specifically: (1) participating States are not required to collect the needed information from recipients to validate compliance assurances or to disclose how compliance was determined; and (2) some, but not all, recipients of SSBCI funds are required to provide compliance assurances.

Participating States are required to provide quarterly assurances to Treasury that State programs approved for SSBCI funding are being implemented in accordance with the requirements of the Act. However, Treasury does not require participating States to collect or disclose the needed information to support those assurances. For example, policy guidelines require that each financial institution lender obtain a certificate of assurance from borrowers affirming that loan proceeds are used for business purposes and are not used for prohibited purposes or provided to ineligible parties. However, financial institutions are not required to report borrower compliance to the participating State entities designated as being responsible for overseeing the participating State programs. Also, participating States do not appear to have an express obligation to collect, or review borrower certificates to ensure that financial institution lenders are fulfilling their obligations under the Act.

As a result, it is unclear what liability there is for a participating State's failure to exercise oversight of the loan-use requirements and restrictions under the policy guidelines if there is no express requirement for financial institution lenders to deliver these assurances to the participating States. The Allocation Agreement requires that each participating State certify it has complied with the covenants and agreements in the Allocation Agreement, including following the policy guidelines, before receiving a disbursement. However, if the participating States are not receiving the information needed to stay informed about whether the borrowers and lenders are complying with the guidelines, they could provide false certifications that would place them in violation of their Allocation Agreements. Further, because lenders and borrowers are not required to report assurances to the participating State, the Treasury OIG may not be able to find the participating State in default for false compliance certifications.

Moreover, the information that financial institutions report to the designated participating State entities bears no relationship to the information that the participating States are required to report to Treasury. Financial institutions primarily collect information about the borrower's business, use of proceeds, and related party transactions, while the participating States collect information relating to whether the lender has made or refinanced loans in order to bring otherwise ineligible loans into the participating State program. As a result, it is not clear whether the scope of assurances to be provided by participating States is limited to just ineligible refinanced loans or whether it also extends to borrower assurances about the use of loan proceeds.

Our review also disclosed that Treasury could do more to strengthen State compliance assurances. Currently, Treasury requires that participating States detail their compliance and oversight regimes in Questions 5a, 5b, and 4h of the program application. However, neither the Allocation Agreement nor the policy guidelines require participating States to disclose what oversight efforts they took in order to provide Treasury with the required compliance assurances. If States were required to disclose their oversight efforts, it would provide Treasury with a stronger basis for determining whether the compliance assurances reported by the participating States are valid. It would also provide Treasury with the information needed to determine whether a participating State has provided a materially false certification.

Finally, the Act and policy guidelines establish reporting requirements for financial institutions, but are silent as to what information is required to be reported by State-sponsored venture capital organizations and other recipients that are not financial institutions. For example, venture capital organizations are permissible participants in Other Credit Support Programs, but it is not clear how the affirmations regarding loan use would apply to them, since the types of investments they make may not necessarily qualify as loans. Without assurances from State-sponsored venture capital organizations, participating States may certify that all recipients of its programs are complying with SSBCI requirements without knowing whether they do.

Treasury Has Not Defined What Constitutes a Material Adverse Change for Purposes of Declaring an Event of Default

One of the covenants in the Allocation Agreement requires participating States to inform Treasury if there is a material adverse change in the participating State's condition, financial or otherwise, or operations. However, Treasury has not defined "material adverse change," creating uncertainty about what constitutes such a change and when a participating State must notify Treasury. It also has implications for a participating State's pre-disbursement certification.

Participating States must certify before each disbursement that they are generally in compliance with SSBCI program requirements. However, since Treasury has not defined a "material adverse change," a participating State may unknowingly experience such a change, and make a false certification that there have been no such changes in its condition, financial or otherwise, or operations, which could cause an event of default. Treasury would also be unable to hold the State accountable for failure to report a "material adverse change."

Treasury officials believe that in both instances these were minor drafting errors, and readily agreed that they should be fixed.

Recommendations

We recommend that the Deputy Assistant Secretary for Small Business, Housing and Community Development (SBH&CD):

1) Define supervision, oversight, and accounting; and set minimum standards for participating State oversight of SSBCI recipients, including defining a participating State's role in overseeing compliance with loan- use requirements and restrictions.

Management Response

The Deputy Assistant Secretary for SBH&CD concurred with the recommendation, and stated that the Frequently Asked Questions (FAQs) for SSBCI will be amended to include a section that will combine all applicable oversight requirements in one place. Additionally, the FAQs will elaborate on the specific duty that each provision imposes upon the participating State. Further, Treasury will publish national compliance standards, which will establish a common set of minimal baseline requirements for participating States as they establish and oversee compliance and reporting responsibilities. The standards will also recommend best practices to enhance participating States' compliance regimes. Once the standards are finalized, Treasury will develop a communications plan to ensure that participating States and known third party stakeholders are aware of the standards. The Deputy Assistant Secretary also stated that he welcomes additional OIG commentary as the standards are developed.

OIG Comments

We consider Treasury's planned actions to be responsive to our recommendation. However, Treasury will need to establish a definitive date for completing its planned actions.

2) Specify what "answerable to" the designated State agencies means relative to the waterfall agreement provision in Annex 1 to the Allocation Agreement.

Management Response

The Deputy Assistant Secretary for SBH&CD agreed to clarify what "answerable to" means by publishing an FAQ that clarifies when a third party is not a direct successor in interest to a participating State. Additionally, the FAQ will put applicants and participating States on notice that Treasury requires a waterfall provision in Allocation Agreements with participating States that use third party entities. Further, the FAQ will establish that, when a participating State proposes to change its program structure in a way that makes use of third party entities, the participating State must notify Treasury and seek a modification of its Allocation Agreement.

OIG Comments

We consider Treasury's planned action to be responsive to our recommendation. However, Treasury will need to establish a definitive date for completing its planned actions.

3) Either modify the Allocation Agreement or amend the policy guidelines to require participating States to make a representation that it is aware of, monitoring, and enforcing compliance with the policy guidelines and other restrictions applicable to program recipients.

Management Response

The Deputy Assistant Secretary for SBH&CD agreed that States must be aware of, monitor, and enforce compliance with SSBCI policy guidelines, but did not agree that additional requirements needed to be established. He stated that States must submit quarterly reports, certifying that they are implementing their programs in accordance with the SSBCI requirements. Therefore, he believes the certification provides an adequate assurance that each State is aware of, monitoring, and enforcing compliance with Treasury's requirements. However, the Deputy Assistant Secretary stated that he appreciates the OIG's concerns and will continue working with the OIG to further strengthen and improve the existing oversight regime.

OIG Comments

We do not consider management's comments to be responsive to the intent of the recommendation. Under program requirements, the State has primary responsibility for ensuring compliance with requirements governing how the SSBCI funds are to be used. Although participating States are required to quarterly certify that they are complying with requirements for the SSBCI program, State certifications could be based solely on compliance assurances received from financial institutions and borrowers without any monitoring or verification by the State of that compliance. Therefore, requiring each participating State to affirmatively certify that it is aware of, and is monitoring and enforcing compliance with the funding restrictions and requirements placed on recipients would provide Treasury some assurance that States are providing the supervision of recipients intended by Treasury guidance. Additionally, such a certification would strengthen Treasury's ability to hold States accountable for recipients' actions should the OIG identify any instances of reckless or intentional misuse of program funds. We will continue to work with Treasury to strengthen and improve the existing oversight regime and plan to pursue resolution of the recommendation through the audit resolution process.

4) Either modify the Allocation Agreement or amend the policy guidelines to define the terms, "intentional or reckless misuse of allocated funds."

Management Response

The Deputy Assistant Secretary for SBH&CD concurred with the recommendation. He stated that Treasury will publish an FAQ to clarify that any use of funds that is inconsistent with current policy guidelines and FAQs will qualify as "misuse." The FAQ will also provide illustrations of conduct that qualifies as intentional or reckless misuse.

OIG Comments

We consider Treasury's planned action to be responsive to the recommendation. However, Treasury will also need to establish a definitive date for completing its planned action.

5) Require that borrowers and lenders provide compliance assurances to the designated State agency responsible for administering the SSBCI funds, and require that the participating States review borrower and lender compliance assurances.

Management Response

The Deputy Assistant Secretary for SBH&CD concurred with the recommendation and agreed to clarify in the forthcoming national compliance standards Treasury's expectations for review of lender certifications. In addition, the standards will address the responsibility of participating States to establish a process to review and assess the validity of borrower certifications.

OIG Comments

We consider Treasury's planned actions to be responsive to the recommendation. However, Treasury will also need to establish a definitive date for completing its planned actions.

6) Clarify whether the scope of assurances to be provided by participating States extend to borrower assurances about the use of loan proceeds.

Management Response

The Deputy Assistant Secretary for SBH&CD concurred with the recommendation, but noted that processes needed for participating States to make a representation that assurances are factually accurate are beyond the framework contemplated by the Act. Nevertheless, he stated that Treasury will clarify in the forthcoming national compliance standards that States must establish a procedure to review and assess the validity of the assurances it collects from borrowers and lenders. The standards will also include guidance on ways that participating States may use these assurances, combined with compliance monitoring controls, to establish a reasonable basis upon which to make assurances to Treasury.

OIG Comments

We consider Treasury's planned actions to be responsive to the recommendation. However, Treasury will need to establish a definitive date for completing its planned actions.

7) Require that participating States disclose what oversight efforts it took in order to provide Treasury with the required program compliance assurances.

Management Response

The Deputy Assistant Secretary for SBH&CD concurred with the recommendation. He stated that based on the OIG's previous feedback, in April 2011 Treasury modified the SSBCI application to require that applicants detail their oversight and compliance regimes prior to receiving program approval. This information combined with SSBCI loan use requirements, sex-offender certifications, and compliance waterfall provisions, will ensure that Treasury is well informed about participating States' oversight efforts. However, Treasury will further clarify this issue in the forthcoming national compliance standards. He also stated that Treasury welcomes additional input from the OIG on this point as the national compliance standards take shape.

OIG Comments

We commend Treasury for modifying the SSBCI application earlier this year to require that applicants detail their oversight plans prior to being accepted into the program. We believe that Treasury's planned actions are needed because they will help Treasury determine the extent to which participants executed their planned oversight regimes detailed in their applications. We consider Treasury's proposed actions to be responsive to the recommendation. However, Treasury will need to establish a definitive date for completing its planned actions.

8) Establish reporting requirements for recipients that are not financial institutions and extend loan restrictions identified in policy guidelines to all potential recipients, such as venture capital organizations.

Management Response

The Deputy Assistant Secretary for SBH&CD concurred with the recommendation and agreed to revise the policy guidelines as recommended.

OIG Comments

We consider Treasury's planned action to be responsive to the recommendation. However, Treasury will need to establish a definitive date for revising the guidelines.

9) Define the term "material adverse change" so that a participating State will know when it must inform Treasury of changes in its condition, financial or otherwise, or operations.

Management Response

The Deputy Assistant Secretary concurred with the recommendation. He stated that Treasury will publish an FAQ that will provide the participating States clarification of the meaning of "material adverse change" for purposes of the notification requirement under the Allocation Agreement. A material adverse change will be triggered by six events. Additionally, this FAQ will serve as interpretive guidance to the program.

OIG Comments

We consider Treasury's planned action to be responsive to the recommendation. However, Treasury will need to establish a definitive date for implementing its proposed action.

* * * * * *

We appreciate the courtesies and cooperation provided to our staff during the evaluation. If you wish to discuss the report, you may contact me at (202) 622-1090 or Lisa DeAngelis, Audit Director, at (202) 927-5621.

/s/

Debra Ritt
Special Deputy Inspector General for
Office of Small Business Lending Fund Program Oversight

We conducted an evaluation of the State Small Business Credit Initiative (SSBCI) Allocation Agreement between the Treasury Department (Department) and participating States and the Department's *Guidelines for State Small Business Credit Initiative* (policy guidelines) for SSBCI. The Small Business Jobs Act directs the Office of Small Business Lending Fund Program Oversight within the Treasury Office of Inspector General (OIG) to conduct and coordinate audits and investigations of the policies, procedures and use of SSBCI funds made available to participating states and municipalities. The OIG will report to the Secretary of the Treasury and Congress on the results of oversight activities, including recommended program improvements.

At the time of tour evaluation, Treasury had established an allocation agreement and policy guidelines to ensure participating States were compliant with requirements of the program. We reviewed the documents to determine whether Treasury had adequately defined the compliance and oversight obligations of participating States to establish proper accountability for oversight of allocated funds. Therefore, our review focused on the Allocation Agreement, policy guidelines, annexes, appendices, and supplements to the Allocation Agreement, Frequently Asked Questions and the Allocation Notice Agreement.

We planned and performed the evaluation to obtain sufficient, appropriate evidence to provide a reasonable basis for our findings and conclusions based on our objectives. We believe that the evidence obtained provides a reasonable basis for our findings and conclusions based on our evaluation objectives.

We performed this evaluation in accordance with the Quality Standards for Inspection and Evaluation, issued by the Council of the Inspectors General on Integrity and Efficiency. Consistent with the evaluation objectives, we did not assess SSBCI's overall internal control or management control structure, obtain data from their information systems or assess the effectiveness of their information system controls. In addition, we did not perform a detailed compliance review of all of the Small Business Jobs Act requirements.

DEPARTMENT OF THE TREASURY
WASHINGTON, D.C. 20220

August 5, 2011

Debra Ritt
Special Deputy Inspector General for
Office of Small Business Lending Fund Program Oversight
U.S. Department of the Treasury
1500 Pennsylvania Avenue, NW
Washington, DC 20220

Dear Ms. Ritt:

Thank you for the opportunity to review your draft report regarding the compliance and
oversight obligations of states participating in the State Small Business Credit Initiative (SSBCI).

Enclosed please find our responses to the recommendations in the draft report. We appreciate
the valuable feedback your team has offered throughout the course of this audit, and look
forward to continued collaboration as the SSBCI program moves forward.

Sincerely,

Don Graves Jr.
Deputy Assistant Secretary for Small Business,
Community Development, and Affordable
Housing Policy

Management Responses to draft OIG recommendations:

1) **Define supervision and oversight and accountability; and set minimum standards for participating State oversight of SSBCI recipients, including defining a participating State's role in overseeing compliance with loan use requirements and restrictions.**

Management Response

Treasury appreciates this guidance from the OIG and agrees that participating States should have a clear understanding of their obligation to oversee SSBCI funds. Currently, the *Guidelines for State Small Business Credit Initiative* ("Policy Guidelines"), Allocation Agreement, and SSBCI Frequently Asked Questions document ("FAQs") delineate a State's responsibility for oversight of loan use requirements and restrictions. In order to enhance a State's understanding of these existing requirements, Treasury will add a section to the FAQs that will collect all applicable oversight requirements in one place. The FAQ will also elaborate on the specific duty each provision imposes upon the participating State.

Further, Treasury will publish national compliance standards pursuant to Section 4.6(a) of the Allocation Agreement and Section 3009 of the Small Business Jobs Act. While each participating State differs in the design and implementation of its program, these national compliance standards will establish a common set of minimal baseline requirements for participating States as they establish and oversee compliance and reporting responsibilities. Among other things, these national standards will address:

- Oversight of lender and investor compliance and reporting responsibilities
- State responsibility for loan-use and sex-offender certifications
- State responsibility for the oversight and compliance of contractors
- Documentation of certain internal controls and procedures

The national compliance standards will also recommend best practices to enhance participating States' compliance regimes.

Once the national compliance standards are finalized, Treasury will develop a communication plan to ensure that participating States and known third party stakeholders are aware of the standards. Treasury expects to disseminate the standards to the Authorized State Officials who oversee the participating State programs and individuals who manage the approved programs on a day-to-day basis. Additionally, Treasury plans to publish a "Notice of Availability" in the Federal Register that will direct stakeholders to the SSBCI website to view the national compliance standards. Treasury also anticipates hosting "town hall" conference calls with participating States in order to provide notice of the standards, discuss the content of the standards, and to answer any questions.

Treasury has already discussed the preliminary elements of these minimum national standards with OIG, and welcomes additional OIG commentary as the document develops.

1

2) **Specify what "answerable to" the designated Sate agencies means relative to the waterfall agreement provision in Annex 1 to the Allocation Agreement.**

Management Response

Treasury includes a waterfall provision in Annex 1 to the Allocation Agreement when the entity administering an SSBCI-approved program (as identified in Section 1D of the Application) is not a direct successor in interest to the entity implementing the program (as identified in Section 1B of the Application and 5.1 of the Allocation Agreement). The waterfall provision requires any entity that is not a direct successor in interest to the participating State, but is nonetheless involved in the administration of the approved program, to adhere to the loan purpose requirements, general default provisions, and other applicable provisions of the Allocation Agreement. A third party entity is not a direct successor in interest to a participating State when the entity's existence does not rely on the participating State's appropriated funds to operate, or its management is not appointed by or subject to removal by the participating State, or it was not created by the participating State's legislation, or it is a for-profit or non-profit entity.

Treasury agrees that SSBCI applicants and participating States should be on notice that Treasury requires a waterfall provision in Allocation Agreements with participating States that use third party entities. Accordingly, Treasury will draft an FAQ to explain this point. The FAQ will also clarify the standard Treasury uses to determine that a third party entity is not a direct successor in interest to a participating State. Additionally, the FAQ will establish that, when a participating State proposes to change its program structure in a way that makes use of third party entities, the participating State must notify Treasury and seek a modification of its Allocation Agreement.

3) **Either modify the Allocation Agreement or amend the policy guidelines to require participating States to make a representation that it is aware of, monitoring and enforcing compliance with the policy guidelines and other restrictions applicable to the other participants in the program.**

Treasury agrees that States must be aware of, monitor, and enforce compliance with SSBCI Policy Guidelines and other relevant restrictions. For this reason, Section 4.6 of the Allocation Agreement mandates that States comply with the Policy Guidelines and any national standards Treasury might establish. Section 4.7 requires a participating State to submit quarterly reports to Treasury that include, among other things, a certification that the participating State is "implementing its Approved State Program or Programs in accordance with the Act and the regulations or other guidance issued by Treasury under the Act." Treasury believes that this certification provides a reasonable assurance that the participating State is aware of, monitoring, and enforcing compliance with program requirements. Nonetheless, Treasury appreciates OIG's concern and will continue working with OIG to further strengthen and improve the existing oversight regime.

4) **Either modify the Allocation Agreement or amend the policy guidelines to define the terms, "intentional or reckless misuse of allocated funds."**

Treasury appreciates the OIG's feedback on this point, and agrees that it should provide additional clarity on what qualifies as "intentional or reckless misuse of allocated funds."

2

Currently, the Policy Guidelines and FAQs set out eligible uses of SSBCI funds, program income, and loan proceeds, and also define eligible borrowers. Treasury will publish an FAQ to clarify that any use of funds that is inconsistent with these provisions qualifies as "misuse." The FAQ will also provide illustrations of conduct that qualifies as intentional misuse and reckless misuse. Once this FAQ is in place, Treasury believes that participating States and third party stakeholders will have a clear understanding of how Treasury will apply the "intentional or reckless misuse" standard. Treasury welcomes input from OIG as it develops the illustrations in the FAQ.

5) **Require that borrowers and lenders provide compliance assurances to the designated State agency responsible for administering the SSBCI funds, and require that the participating States review them.**

Treasury agrees that it should clarify a participating State's responsibilities related to borrower and lender assurances, and will address this issue in the forthcoming national compliance standards. Currently, borrowers must certify to lenders that they have used loan proceeds in a manner consistent with the Policy Guidelines. In turn, lenders must make their own assurances to participating States concerning loan proceeds. To facilitate this process, Treasury created sample self-certifications that lenders may use to obtain certifications from borrowers, and that participating States may use to obtain certifications from lenders. Although the requirement that lenders provide assurances to participating States implies that participating States should review those assurances, Treasury agrees that it currently does not explicitly mandate such a review. The national compliance standards will clarify Treasury's expectations for review of lender certifications. The standards will also address participating States' responsibility to establish a process to review and assess the validity of borrower certifications. Treasury will continue working with OIG as it develops these standards.

6) **Clarify whether the scope of assurances to be provided by participating States extends to borrower assurances about the use of loan proceeds.**

The scope of State certification on use-of-funds is set out in Annex 4 of the Allocation Agreement at Exhibit 4-1, and does not encompass borrower assurances about the use of loan and investment proceeds. In order for participating States to make a representation that borrower assurances are factually accurate, participating States would be required to independently validate each lender, investor, and borrower certification for each dollar loaned or invested under the SSBCI program. Such a process would be beyond the framework contemplated by Section 3005(e) of the Small Business Jobs Act of 2010, which establishes a system of lender and borrower self-certifications as the primary means of monitoring a borrower's use of SSBCI proceeds.

Nevertheless, participating States must ensure that loan use requirements are met. Treasury requires participating States to use both borrower to lender, and lender to participating State certifications along with program-specific compliance mechanisms to establish a basis for participating State assurances to Treasury. Treasury's national compliance standards will clarify that States must establish a procedure to review and assess the validity of the assurances it collects from borrowers and lenders. Treasury will also provide guidance on ways that

3

participating States may use these assurances, combined with compliance monitoring controls, to establish a reasonable basis upon which to make assurances to Treasury.

7) Require that participating States disclose what oversight efforts it took in order to provide Treasury with the required program compliance assurances.

In response to valuable feedback from OIG, Treasury modified the SSBCI application in April 2011 to require that applicants detail their oversight and compliance regimes prior to receiving approval for participation in the program. Applicants must now set out their existing and planned compliance efforts in questions 4H, 5A, and 5B. These responses are rated as a part of Treasury's application approval process, and insufficient responses are referred back to the participating State for more information. The responses are then incorporated by reference into the Allocation Agreement between Treasury and the participating State. This process, combined with SSBCI loan use requirements, sex-offender certifications, and compliance waterfall provisions, ensures that Treasury is well informed about participating States' oversight efforts. However, Treasury will further clarify this issue in the forthcoming national compliance standards. Treasury welcomes additional input from OIG on this point as the national compliance standards take shape.

8) Establish reporting requirements for recipients that are not financial institutions and extend loan restrictions identified in policy guidelines to all potential recipients, such as venture capital organizations.

Treasury appreciates this recommendation from the OIG and will revise the Policy Guidelines to address both points. Treasury intended that most reporting requirements and loan restrictions in the SSBCI Policy Guidelines, Allocation Agreement, and FAQs related to *loans* also apply to *investments* made under an approved venture capital program. While Section 4.8 of the Allocation Agreement currently requires that participating States submit annual reports to Treasury for all loans and investments, regardless of whether the lender is a financial institution or other type of eligible investor, Treasury agrees that the Policy Guidelines do not consistently extend these obligations to all potential recipients. Treasury will revise the Policy Guidelines to clarify that when a State's approved program involves recipients that are not financial institution lenders, such as venture capital organizations, the State is bound by the same reporting requirements and loan restrictions as it would be for loan proceeds.

9) Define the term "material adverse change" so that participating States will know when they must inform Treasury of changes in its financial operational condition.

Treasury appreciates this recommendation from the OIG and agrees that it should provide participating States with clarification of the meaning of "material adverse change." Accordingly, Treasury will publish an FAQ stating that, for the purposes of the Allocation Agreement, the notice requirement of Section 4.10(b) of the Allocation Agreement is triggered by the following events:

1) The elimination or termination of an Approved State Program;

4

2) The addition of one or more new State programs;

3) A material change in the scope or purpose of an Approved State Program. Treasury maintains the discretion to determine materiality of any changes in scope or purposes that are proposed by a Participating State;

4) The reapportionment and transfer of a Participating State's allocated funds among Approved State Programs, when the cumulative amounts transferred exceeds 10 percent of the Participating State's total allocation;

5) A change in the identity of the State agency or contracting entity proposed to implement the Approved State Programs from the State agency that is identified in Section 5.1 or Annex 1 of the Allocation Agreement or a merger of State agencies or contracting entities is proposed that substantially alters the organizational structure of the implementing Participating State agency or contracting entity; or

6) Extenuating circumstances requiring extensions to the reporting schedule established in Annex 5 of the Allocation Agreement.

These six events are drawn from the SSBCI Modification Policy. This FAQ will serve as interpretive guidance to the program.

5

Department of the Treasury
Deputy Secretary
Office of Strategic Planning and Performance Management
Office of Accounting and Internal Control

Office of Management and Budget
OIG Budget Examiner

United States Senate
Chairman and Ranking Member
Committee on Small Business and Entrepreneurship

Chairman and Ranking Member
Committee on Finance

Chairman and Ranking Member
Committee on Banking, Housing and Urban Affairs

United States House of Representatives
Chairman and Ranking Member
Committee on Small Business

Chairman and Ranking Member
Committee on Financial Services

Government Accountability Office
Comptroller General of the United States